Aung San Suu Kyi

Aung San Suu Kyi

Politician, Prisoner, Parent

Wendy Law-Yone

TLS

TLS Books
An imprint of HarperCollins*Publishers*
1 London Bridge Street
London SE1 9GF

The-TLS.co.uk

HarperCollins*Publishers*
Macken House, 39/40 Mayor Street Upper,
Dublin 1 D01 C9W8, Ireland

First published in Great Britain in 2023 by TLS Books

1

A catalogue record for this book is
available from the British Library

ISBN 978-0-00-854130-9

Typeset in Publico Text
Printed and bound in the UK using 100%
renewable electricity at CPI Group (UK) Ltd

MIX
Paper | Supporting
responsible forestry
FSC™ C007454

This book is produced from independently certified FSC™ paper
to ensure responsible forest management.

For more information visit: www.harpercollins.co.uk/green

For 'Htan Thee' and 'Lone Lone'
and for **Gen Z**

In September 2012, at an Amnesty International event held in her honour in Washington, DC, Aung San Suu Kyi, Nobel Peace Prize laureate and Amnesty's Ambassador of Conscience, was presented with a bouquet by a little Russian girl. The girl's mother was Nadezhda Tolokonnikova, founder of the punk band Pussy Riot, who with two other bandmates was serving out a harsh term in a Siberian labour camp for the 'hooliganism' of a protest song staged at Moscow's main Russian Orthodox cathedral. The song was called 'Punk Prayer: Mother of God, Drive Putin Away'.

Suu Kyi accepted the flowers seemingly unaware of the identity of the little girl, Gera Verzilov, who happened to be on a media tour of the USA with her father, Pyotr. Pyotr had described to the press how, earlier that week, Gera visited her mother in prison for the first time in six months, and afterwards sent her sketches with plans for her escape from prison.

No mention was made of Pussy Riot until towards the end of the programme, when one of the students in the audience invited Suu Kyi to comment on the cause célèbre.

'Well, I don't see why people shouldn't sing whatever it is that they want to sing,' said Suu Kyi. 'There's nothing wrong with singing. I think the only reason why people should not sing is if what they're saying is deliberately insulting ... or if they sing terribly ... that would be the best reason for not singing at all.' After the laughter had died down, she concluded, 'So I would like the whole group to be released as soon as possible.'

One of the event moderators asked a follow-up question: whether Suu Kyi had a specific message for the Russian government regarding Pussy Riot. Her response: 'I want to ask one question first. Was there anything in the songs that was nasty to other people?' The moderator conceded that it was a matter of judgment; people could take offence.

'When you say people,' Suu Kyi inquired further, 'do you mean the government?' When the moderator said yes, her reply was: 'Well I think governments don't count as people.'

Laughter and applause from the audience.[1]

* * *

Six years later, on 11 November 2018, Amnesty International informed Aung San Suu Kyi in an open letter: 'You no longer represent a symbol of hope, courage, and the undying defence of human rights. Amnesty International cannot justify your continued status as a recipient of the Ambassador of Conscience Award and so with great sadness we are hereby withdrawing it from you.'[2]

1.

My first and only close encounter with Aung San Suu Kyi was a quasi-religious experience. The occasion was a literature festival, but because we were in Myanmar, and in Myanmar important Buddhist feast days are cause for carnival, this event had the familiar feel of a temple fair. There were marquees for celebrity preachers and their followers; food stalls serving samosas and sweet tea; vendors of cultural curios and sacred ephemera, and saffron-robed monks sifting through the cornucopia of books for the taking. There were dancing girls and strolling nuns, and a large video screen with soundless loops of festival highlights happening elsewhere.

The only thing missing was turtles. When I was a child growing up in Rangoon, sacred turtles roamed the grounds of pagodas and other pilgrimage sites, giving rise to the expression 'digging for turtle eggs while worshipping at the shrine' to describe the killing of two birds with one stone, or, put another way, the habit of praying a little, playing a little, on the path to salvation.

But this was no garden-variety temple fair, nor was it your run-of-the-mill book fair. This was an *international* literary festival, only the second of its kind to be allowed in a country just emerging from decades of draconian repression and censorship. Also, it was taking place in Mandalay, the old royal capital, a city second in size to Rangoon (now Yangon) but not in historic or cultural significance.

The inaugural festival, held in Yangon the previous year, had 'achieved more for freedom of speech in one afternoon than most of us manage in a lifetime', in the giddy words of William Hague, the then Foreign Secretary. And the festival's official patron was none other than the world's most celebrated champion of democracy, Aung San Suu Kyi.

Recently liberated from her latest detention – from a combined total of fifteen years over the previous two decades – Daw (honorific) Suu would be arriving in person to give her blessing to this, the 2014 Irrawaddy Literary Festival, where a former BBC journalist would be interviewing her onstage.

As one of the dozens of writers flown in from distant lands (the UK in my case) to attend the festival, I was entitled to a seat at this exclusive event and arrived at the venue in plenty of time to beat the crowds. Or so I thought. Instead I ran into a flash mob swarming the grounds of the Mandalay Hill Resort Hotel, where the festival was being held.

Outside the building where Daw Suu was scheduled to speak, an unruly queue of ticket-holders and gatecrashers was muscling its way in through the main entrance. I fell in, or rather was pushed in by a festival organiser standing by for the purpose, like one of those white-gloved Tokyo subway attendants tasked with cramming rush-hour commuters into overcrowded trains.

The queue I was now trapped in moved slowly and in lockstep, despite much bumping and shoving and other underhand acts of aggression. But, once past the entrance, things came to a standstill. There was no place to go: no way past the bodies bottlenecking the doorway to the lecture room within. And no way past the bodies piling in thick and fast from the rear. There was only one solution to the obstruction, and we, the entitled mob, went for it. Heaving and hoing, we stormed the inner entrance as one big battering ram until a sudden body-slam sent me clear past the bottleneck and into the room. I was in!

Standing room only didn't describe the half of it. People were sharing chairs, leaning against walls, hogging every square inch of available floor space. I looked around helplessly and caught the eye of another festival guest who gestured to the half-hidden empty seat next to his. Running the gauntlet of knees and book bags blocking the way, I grabbed it.

A chorus of loud shushes called for silence. An obedient hush descended, lasting only a moment. Then Aung San Suu Kyi came through the door, a vision in silk the colour of old polished silver, and the audience gasped and rose to their feet.

The Burmese word for a certain kind of charisma is *awza*. A person in possession of *awza* exudes authority without the need to exert power or force in any overt way. In trying to capture the *awza* of a person who brings an audience, any audience, to its feet just by entering a room, I am reminded of Turgenev's example of a less-is-more approach to narrative description. 'Do you remember', he wrote, 'the way Homer conveys Helen's beauty? With these simple words: "When Helen walked in, at the sight of her beauty old men rose to their feet."'

Old men reportedly rose to their feet when Aung San Suu Kyi entered the courtroom to which she was once summoned during her long imprisonment – old men in military garb who nevertheless went on to prolong her incarceration for yet another indefinite term.

The applause died down only after Daw Suu and her interviewer, Joan Bakewell, had settled into their seats. My own seat did not allow a frontal view of the speakers. Disappointingly, it was placed at a 45-degree angle to the rear. But never mind. I could at least admire the faint ikat print on the silk of Daw Suu's matching *longyi*, *aingyi* and shawl, and her signature hair ornament of fresh flowers (blood-red roses in this instance).

Three years had passed since Aung San Suu Kyi's release from house arrest. In the meantime, she had toured the world making speeches and collecting awards she hadn't been able to accept during her years under detention – the 1991 Nobel Peace Prize, for instance – and her once-rare interviews had lost some of their novelty. This one was proceeding more or less as expected: a repertoire of respectful questions countered with a repertoire of stock answers, by turns pithy and dismissive.

Asked about the writers she admired, the Lady (as she was popularly known at the time) named some of her old college favourites, among them Charles Dickens and Jane Austen. No mention was made of any Burmese writers, past or present. Or absent; a number of established writers, from both Yangon and Mandalay, had boycotted the festival on grounds of discrimination, or disrespect, or both, by the British festival organisers; but of this contretemps the festival's Burmese patron seemed unaware.

Then came the obligatory interview question of a thorny nature: the matter of escalating anti-Muslim violence stoked by Burmese Buddhist fundamentalists. The Lady's response was short, sharp and ecumenical. Christians misbehaved too, she said.

I was having trouble concentrating on the interview because the scrimmage outside had left me with a headache. I felt a migraine coming on. The dread signs were impossible to ignore: nausea, throbbing eye sockets, an aura of pulsing lights and foggy shapes. As I focused my gaze on the faces of the audience across from me, what came to mind was an early Bill Viola video installation.

It was the one called *Sea of Silence*: a ten-minute video, projected on a giant screen, of a dozen or so people standing side by side, watching something ineffable take place in front of them: something we, the audience, cannot see. All we see is a sequence of intense but unfathomable expressions passing over their faces, each new expression unfolding in torturous slow motion, yet never revealing the *mysterium tremendum et fascinans* occurring off-screen.

I snapped out of my migraine-induced fugue only when the audience rose to their feet once again and I realised the interview was over.

I dashed for the exit, desperate for the balm of silence and darkness, and was back in my hotel room, burrowed into bed, when I heard the commotion: cheers and chants and car horns that sounded like the victory celebration of a national football team. It was only much later, watching video replays of the festival highlights, that I was able to see, and not just hear, the Lady's ceremony of departure.

She left, it seemed, in much the same way she had arrived: mobbed by ecstatic devotees and encircled in their midst by her security detail, a corps of young NLD members in white jackets, hands locked in daisy-chain formation. The small security group represented the new generation of the National League for Democracy, the political party she had co-founded more than a quarter-century ago – the same NLD which she led to landside electoral victory in 1990.

It was in those videos too that I heard once again what had come through the window of my hotel room as the Lady drove home that afternoon. Not home to Yangon, where she had languished for nearly two decades under house arrest, but to her new home in Naypyidaw, now the capital city of a nation in transition: from military dictatorship to democracy (not any old democracy, mind, but what the generals called 'discipline-flourishing democracy').

'Amay Suu! Amay Suu!' ('Mother Suu! Mother Suu!') I heard, and was struck by how a term of endearment could be turned into a rallying cry, a call to arms. That rallying cry would resound all over the country in the months that followed, in the run-up to the 2015 national elections.

In the event – the first openly contested poll in twenty-five years – it was her party, the NLD, that would win by an overwhelming majority. The victory would elevate

Amay Suu to the position of State Counsellor – a rank that placed her 'above the president', as she herself made clear – an important distinction, given that the military-drafted constitution expressly denied her the presidency on the ground that her two sons, being British citizens, 'owe allegiance to a foreign power'.

Out in the streets, however, no one ever shouted out, 'State Counsellor! State Counsellor!' It was only ever 'Mother Suu! Mother Suu!'.

2.

The mantle of national motherhood had actually been bestowed on Suu Kyi a few years earlier. On Friday, 12 November 2010 a thousand or so people were gathered outside 54 University Avenue, her dilapidated, colonial-era family home on the shore of Inya Lake. The entrance was surrounded by military roadblocks, and ten police trucks idled within spitting distance. Another crowd of almost equal strength had set up camp in front of the headquarters of the NLD on West Shwe Gon Daing Road, where banners and posters featuring their long-imprisoned leader were being put up in a frenzy of anticipation.

No public announcement had been made, but 'it was learned' (as they are wont to say in the state-run Burmese media) that Aung San Suu Kyi was about to be released. Word was that the authorisation papers had been signed, and her arrival was imminent – her first public appearance in seven years.

The crowds were restless but not unruly, consisting mostly of undercover journalists, diplomats, NLD Party stalwarts and unaffiliated fans in T-shirts bearing likenesses of the Lady and 'We Stand With Aung San Suu Kyi' captions. They waited through the day, cameras clicking without hindrance for once, although undercover secret police were duly photographing the photographers, and all over the city riot police were poised for action. But the morning went by, then the afternoon, and still nothing had happened.

It was getting dark by the time U Win Tin, the senior NLD spokesman, arrived at the military roadblock outside the famous prison-home to make an announcement. A former journalist and co-founder of the NLD, 'Hanthawaddy' Win Tin was himself a hero of resistance. While the Lady was confined to her derelict but roomy family home, he was cooped up in Insein Prison, at times in a dog kennel, busy being beaten to a pulp, having his teeth knocked out, losing a testicle as the result of a botched hernia operation in a filthy prison cell, and surviving two heart attacks in between.

The white-haired Win Tin was recognisable by his indigo-blue shirt, the prison-issue uniform he had worn throughout his nineteen-year incarceration and which, even after his release, he would wear every day for the rest of his life as a symbol of resistance.

Yes, Daw Suu had been officially set free, he reported; but no, she wouldn't be appearing till the next morning. She was caught up in last-minute negotiations over the terms of her release, insisting on unconditional freedom of movement once she stepped outside the gate of her prison. Everyone should therefore go home, Win Tin advised, and come back in the morning.

By 11:00 the next morning, on Saturday, 13 November, the military barricades outside Suu Kyi's house had been removed, the riot police recalled, and the thousands of people waiting in the streets were stampeding towards her front gate. And there she was at last, the long-awaited apparition, in a pale-lavender top, fresh flowers in her hair, beaming down at the hordes as she stood on a makeshift platform just high enough for her head and shoulders to rise above the ramparts of her compound's front gate – an impromptu pulpit of sorts. Flanked by two senior NLD associates and a corps of young security guards, she was gripping the bars of her iron gate – the same gate that would be put up for auction at a reserve price of $200,000 a few years later – attempting valiantly to speak to the crowd, but not making much headway with all the cheering and chanting, the screaming of slogans and singing of songs that drowned out whatever she was trying to say.

When at last she was able to make herself heard, at least by the section of the crowd nearest her, it was simply to say, 'It has been a long time, and I have so much to tell you.' Someone reached up to hand her a corsage, with a request that she wear it in her hair. She obliged. Then, realising that trying to speak over the din of jubilation was a lost cause, she invited the crowd to her party headquarters the next day. 'There is a time to be quiet and a time to talk,' she said, a touch of Ecclesiastes in her cadence. A brief call for unity followed ('We must work in unison. Only then will we achieve our goal'), at which the crowds began singing the national anthem.

On the other side of the gate, the Lady stepped down from the table on which she had been standing and strode back to her house, a spring in her step and a swing in her shoulders, a prisoner no more.

'She is our mother, she is our mother!' a woman in the crowd cried.

'Amay Suu, Amay Suu!' another voice proclaimed.

Those cries marked a metamorphosis that had taken place while no one was looking, in the hothouse of prolonged captivity. Twenty years earlier, Aung San Suu Kyi had burst upon the political scene as the daughter of the nation's uncontested hero, General Aung San, and had ended up in isolation soon thereafter. Now she had re-emerged from her cocoon, as mother of her father's nation.

* * *

Two months later, I chanced upon an uncanny illustration of this reassigned parentage, let's call it, while wandering the streets of the Pansodan book district in Rangoon. Aficionados of Pansodan (Myanmar's equivalent of the *Bouquinistes* of Paris, or London's Charing Cross Road back in the day) will be familiar with the thrill of the hunt that comes from sifting through the pay dirt of old textbooks on engineering, medicine, and English grammar; manuals for early IBM word processors and Siemens kitchen appliances, and Buddhist tracts with misleadingly lurid covers – the thrill of sifting through all that dross and finally striking gold with a presentation copy of Leon Uris's *Exodus*, or a spineless paperback of a Danielle Steele novel, or an early edition of Dale Carnegie's *How to Win Friends and Influence People* (a mandatory textbook for Rangoon high school students in the 1950s).

Pansodan on this occasion was awash with fresh merchandise. On display tables, news stands and footstools, on plastic groundsheets and wooden pallets lining the streets were colourful stacks of magazines, newspapers, journals and instant books, all being churned out at speed now that the authorities had eased up on censorship. And on a great many covers was the image of a smiling, waving, radiant Aung San Suu Kyi, always with flowers in her hair.

Here she was, photographed arm in arm with US Secretary of State Hillary Clinton, whose momentous visit had taken place only a week earlier. And there she was, and there, and there, replicated ad infinitum not just on the front pages of papers, but on keychains, pendants, lockets, calendars, fans, wallets ...

The thing that caused me to do a double take, however, was a laminated colour print of Aung San Suu Kyi and her father, General Aung San – not one of the familiar black-and-white snapshots of the daughter as a toddler in her father's arms in the year of his assassination. No, in this portrait – an artefact I kick myself for not acquiring, but still see clearly in my mind's eye – father and daughter are seated side by side. The only odd thing about this family portrait is that General Aung San is thirty-two, the age he was when assassinated, and Aung San Suu Kyi is sixty-six, her actual age – a feat of Photoshop splicing that positions her as the mother, and her eternally youthful father as the son.

Creepy as it seemed to me at the time, this surreal inversion of parentage, so to speak, was just part of the mad rush to rehabilitate Aung San Suu Kyi – by highlighting her exalted pedigree through digital legerdemain. It wasn't so long ago that in the Aung San family portraits sanctioned for public consumption, mother and father were shown with their two small sons, but with the tiny Aung San Suu Kyi, cradled by her mother's arm, excised from the frame altogether.

* * *

The question of lineage and genealogy is ever present in genteel Burmese society. When introduced for the first time to a younger person, it's perfectly acceptable to ask, 'Whose son/daughter are you?' In pedigree is found the true measure and predictor of character – a belief reflected in such proverbs as 'A rotten bamboo can't be sharpened', or 'The trunk confirms an elephant; the nose an Indian'. (A helpful footnote in my old collection of Burmese proverbs explains in English that 'the noses of Indians are more prominent than those of Burmans'.)

The preoccupation with pedigree comes up in saying after saying. A genuine ruby won't sink in the sand. A real chilli pepper will retain its heat, even seven fathoms under water. The word for 'pedigree' being synonymous with the word for 'bone', it follows that 'With a hen it's the bone (structure); with a human it's the kin' which determines good breeding. (*Kyet hmah a yoh; lu hmah a myo*, goes the rhyming couplet in Burmese.) Genealogy, in short, is a matter of kin and bone.

One tricky aspect of establishing genealogy is the impossibility of doing so through family names, for family names are non-existent in Myanmar. The name one is given at birth, usually determined by that particular day of the week, is *sui generis*, self-standing and unchanging, even for a woman when she marries. This is not to say that a person can't assume more than one name over the course of time.

General Aung San's birth name, for example, was Htein Lin ('Bright Light'). But Htein Lin never stuck; it was supplanted early on by Aung San, for reasons Aung San himself was at a loss to explain, since the name 'Aung San' didn't conform, as custom dictated, to the day of the week on which he was born. Later in life, as a member of the legendary Thirty Comrades, the core of the nationalist Burma Independence Army he founded, Aung San assumed yet another name, the *nom de guerre* of Bo Teza. But Aung San was the name that would go down in history.

Most unusually for a Burmese family, however, the children of Aung San, two boys and a girl, all had their father's name affixed to their own at birth. Thus: Aung San Oo, Aung San Lin and Aung San Suu Kyi. This would be akin, in America, to all of Franklin D. Roosevelt's children being named Roosevelt Anna, Roosevelt James, Roosevelt Elliott, Roosevelt John – and perhaps also Roosevelt Franklin Delano Jr – so that each would be known first and foremost as Roosevelt, and only then by his or her other 'first' name.

In the case of the Aung San family, departure from custom suggests that both Aung San and his wife Daw Khin Kyi were prescient about the weight the name Aung San would carry one day. The inherent noblesse oblige would be passed on to their youngest child and only daughter, Aung San Suu Kyi, aged two at the time of her father's assassination.

Suu Kyi grew up with a father both absent and omnipresent. For one thing, her mother made sure he never faded from view – her mother and everyone else. 'People spoke about him all the time. I was told I was his favourite because I was the youngest and only girl.'[3]

'Some would say,' wrote her husband Michael Aris, 'she became obsessed with the image of the father she never knew ... she never for a minute forgot that she was the daughter of Burma's national hero.'[4]

From student leader and anti-colonial activist in the 1930s, Aung San had gone on to spearhead the struggle for independence. At the onset of the Second World War, he collaborated with Japanese plans to invade and 'liberate' Burma from Britain. The colonial police were on to him and put out a warrant for his arrest – adding insult to injury, in the recollection of a fellow comrade, 'by fixing a reward of five rupees for his capture, which was something less, he [Aung San] said bitterly, than the price of a fair-sized chicken. When I mentioned the British, he swore that he would fight them till the end.'[5]

On discovering that the independence promised by the Japanese was specious, however – especially after the Normandy landings put paid to the aims of the Axis – Aung San jumped ship with his newly created Burma

Independence Army and joined the British Allied forces in driving out the Japanese.

Aung San was mistrusted by some in the British government. Winston Churchill called him a dirty word ('quisling') and was affronted by the sight of 'this traitor rebel leader ... marching up the steps of Buckingham Palace as the plenipotentiary of the Burmese Government'.[6] But in the end he gained the grudging respect of the colonial powers and succeeded in negotiating a peaceable end to British rule with Clement Attlee's Labour government. Independence was squarely on its way.

The grisly assassination that cut short General Aung San's stewardship took place only a few months before the transfer of power, in the midst of a meeting with his provisional government. Armed with sub-machine guns, the henchmen of a rival politician were able to burst unhindered into the meeting room at the Secretariat and shoot dead Aung San and most of his cabinet.

That day, 19 July, would be commemorated as Martyrs' Day, a major national holiday. Independence would be declared six months later, on 4 January 1948.

Born in Burma in the year of the momentous assassination, I grew up in the penumbra of General Aung San's heroism and martyrdom. But there came a time when I found the term 'martyr' as applied to Aung San a bit puzzling. 'Hero' I could understand. If our great General Aung San – brave soldier, bold statesman, tragic patriot who never lived to see the freedom he fought so hard for – wasn't a hero, I didn't know who was. But a martyr?

My keen interest in martyrs stemmed from my education at St John's Convent, where the spiritual highlight of each academic year was a retreat. During that retreat, a visiting Redemptorist priest would touch down like a celebrity from outer space to entertain us with hair-curling allegories of mortal sin and its antithesis, martyrdom.

Joan of Arc was a martyr, that was a given: burned at the stake for heresy and mourned for her sacrifice for the French nation. And there was St Sebastian, converter of Roman soldiers to Christianity, shot with arrows that lodged in his flesh but stopped short of killing him (death came only later – by cudgel).

But General Aung San hadn't died in battle, or on the scaffold, in the service of his beliefs. He was mown down in cold blood, not because he was a threat to any ruling orthodoxy or authority but because some petty political rival wanted him dead. Did that make Aung San a martyr?

I can't remember giving much more thought to the question until long after I left Burma in 1967 – much later than that, really. In 2015, while teaching at the University of Berne, I was invited by an Italian anti-fascist foundation in Parma to give a lecture on Aung San. It was the hundredth anniversary of his birthday and the broad-based political party he had instituted – after founding the Communist Party of Burma (CPB) in 1939 – was the Anti-Fascist People's Freedom League (AFPFL), an umbrella front that would dominate Burmese politics through the era of parliamentary democracy, from 1948 to 1962.

In the course of research for my talk in Parma, I came across a useful gloss to the Burmese definition of *martyr* in, of all places, *The Global New Light of Myanmar*, the government mouthpiece. As an effective outlet for state propaganda, *The Global New Light* falls somewhere between the Nazi Party *Völkischer Beobachter* circa 1941 and the press releases of Baghdad Bob, aka Comical Ali, Saddam Hussein's Information Minister in the 1990s – though it isn't nearly as slick as either.

Nevertheless, I find *The Global New Light of Myanmar* worth reading from time to time, even if the effort inevitably brings to mind the scene in *Slumdog Millionaire* where the young Jamal has to jump into an open cesspit to get the celebrity autograph he seeks: you never know what you might find.

In a special issue commemorating the seventieth anniversary of Martyrs' Day, I found this:

A martyr is 'one who voluntarily undergoes sufferings or death for the sake of any great cause or principle'. This is an oversimplified definition of a martyr which one may find in an English dictionary. But in Burmese the equivalent word for martyr is '*ajani*', a derivative of the Pali word '*ajaniya*' meaning 'the one who is born of good breed and knows well'.

Digging deeper into etymology, I learned that the term *ajani* (or *azani* in Burmese) can apply to a man of wisdom and good breeding who does not necessarily die *from*, but dies *in the course of*, some heroic struggle. The defence lawyer of the venerable U Ottama, for instance, was a martyr. U Ottama was a Theravada monk and anti-colonialist rebel in the 1930s. His lawyer U Sein Hla Aung had expired in office and was declared an *azani*, even though the cause of death was dysentery. An even earlier hero of Theravada Buddhism, the Elder Abhaya, was likewise deemed an *azani* after drifting off on his prayer mat into sleep eternal while reciting the sacred laws and scriptures.[7]

Azani, then, could refer to any mortal who died in the line of duty – religious duty, principally – and was of noble predisposition.

When Aung San Suu Kyi made her debut on the political stage, it was under the banner of history and *azani* writ large.

The year was 1988, and Rangoon, the capital city, was in uproar. Demonstrations and other public protests, led mostly by students, were erupting on a scale unseen since the Rangoon University student agitations following General Ne Win's military coup in 1962. Having spent most of her life abroad, Aung San Suu Kyi was living in Oxford and doing an advanced degree at SOAS when she took what she thought would be temporary leave to tend to her sick mother, who had recently suffered a stroke in Rangoon. Thus she happened to be in Burma just as the uprising was gaining momentum.

By the evening of 25 August, word had spread that a VIP would be arriving the next day at the Shwedagon Pagoda to make a speech. The VIP was something of an unknown to the public – she lived in England and was married to an Englishman – but her credentials were otherwise flawless. She was the daughter of General Aung San.

Overnight, the expectant crowds arrived by the thousands with their blankets, bedrolls, mats and portable meals to stake out their seats for the show ahead. By noon the next day, the audience had swollen into a mass rally of half a million.

The slight, plainly dressed young woman finally ushered onstage by a retinue of student activists could have passed for a student herself. Some years later, one of her closest colleagues, a senior NLD strategist, would recall his first impressions of her back in 1986. 'She seemed like a decent girl who had no interest in frivolous talk or gossip. In fact, I remember thinking how peculiar it was that I never saw her laugh at that time, or it could have been that she didn't want to communicate with strangers ... She didn't impress me at all. Except by how young she looked. She must have been about forty-two at the time, but she could have passed as a girl of seventeen.'[8]

Once the girlish Aung San Suu Kyi stepped up to the stand of microphones onstage, however, she took charge with the confidence of a seasoned public speaker, introducing herself in the direct, unvarnished language for which her famous father had been renowned.

A number of people are saying that since I've spent most of my life abroad and am married to a foreigner, I could not be familiar with ... this country's politics. I wish to speak to you very frankly and openly. It's true that I've lived abroad. It's also true that I'm married to a foreigner. But these facts have never, and will never, interfere with or lessen my love and devotion for my country by any measure or degree.

People have been saying that I know nothing of Burmese politics. The trouble is that I know too much. My family knows best how complicated and tricky Burmese politics can be and how much my father had to suffer on this account.[9]

On the stage, to her right, was a floor-to-ceiling silk-screen poster of General Aung San in pop-art hues. Stretched across the wall behind her was a flag – a white star on a crimson field – that harked back to the General's Second World War resistance days.

Suu Kyi went on to speak of her father's fight for democracy and freedom; of the army he had envisioned – an army that stood for democratic reform, not repression; of the struggle that lay ahead, which amounted to 'the second struggle for national independence'.

For an opening act, Suu Kyi's performance was a tour de force of stage management in another historic sense: it was set in the grounds of the peerless Shwedagon Pagoda. It wasn't only that so many political protests, rebellions and mass rallies had been staged there all through the colonial and the independence eras. The Shwedagon was where sacred relics some 2,500 years old were enshrined, encased in gold and imbued with immortal significance for the Buddhist nation.

Aung San Suu Kyi's Shwedagon speech was followed by a tour of the country during which she addressed nearly a thousand demonstrations and political meetings, calling for democracy and the pursuit of human rights through non-violent civil disobedience.

By September that year, the popular protests sweeping the country had cohered into a mass uprising and then a general strike, increasingly joined by members of the armed forces, but ending in a blood-soaked crackdown. Led by Chief of Staff General Saw Maung, the army began opening fire on demonstrators, killing thousands and driving thousands more into hiding or exile.

Aung San Suu Kyi, leader of the newly formed NLD, was arrested on 20 July 1989 – one day after the forty-second anniversary of her father's assassination. She would spend most of the next two decades in detention.

3.

'What else can one do,' asks Martin Luther King in his *Letter from Birmingham Jail*, 'when he is alone in a narrow jail cell, other than write long letters, think long thoughts and pray long prayers?'

Aung San Suu Kyi could have told him what else one can do in jail: meditate.

In 1995, not long after her release from her first six years under house arrest, Suu Kyi granted a series of interviews to Alan Clements, an American Buddhist who had been ordained a monk in Burma.

'A lot of our people meditate when they're in prison,' she explained, 'partly because they have the time, and partly because it's a very sensible thing to do ... if you have no contact with the outside world, and you can't do anything for it, then you do what you can with the world inside you in order to bring it under proper control.'[10]

Put in such practical terms, the case for meditating in prison could as well be made for basket-weaving, but it was yet another example of Suu Kyi's facility for plain speech, an ability to make even the esoteric seem routine. Equally, she could speak of the spiritual dividends of imprisonment in more ecstatic terms, as in: 'Political prisoners have known the most sublime moments of perfect communion with their highest ideals during periods when they were incarcerated in isolation, cut off from contact with all that was familiar and dear to them.'[11]

The experience of prison as an opportunity for religious contemplation was not, of course, exclusive to Burmese prisoners. Prisons in colonial Indochina, for example, had served a similar politico-spiritual purpose, as recounted by the historian David G. Marr. 'They forced a significant segment of the Vietnamese intelligentsia to withdraw from the world, endure privation, sort out their thoughts and attempt to master the self and external reality. In this sense, prisons were not unlike Zen monasteries, except that the acolytes were not there by choice and those in charge were not seen as teachers but as the enemy.'[12]

The Buddha himself, prior to enlightenment, was thought to have discovered *vipassanā*, making it the oldest expression of Theravada 'mental culture', as some scholars call it. The Vipassanā Movement – with its secular offshoot, the 'mindfulness' prescriptions and therapies of our times – emerged in colonial Burma as a cultural response to the threats posed to Buddhism by a secular British regime on the one hand, and missionary Christianity on the other. The movement became widespread thanks in part to the technologies of mass publishing. Vipassanā was further popularised in the 1950s by the teachings of meditation masters like Mahasi Sayadaw, S.N. Goenka and the lay practitioner Sayagyi U Ba Khin, who was also the Accountant-General of Burma.

It was the militant Burmese nationalist monks of the 1920s, however, who set the tone for Aung San's political rhetoric at independence, with its reliance on Buddhist tropes. As anthropologist Gustaaf Houtman argues, the term *lut-lak-yei* 'was used to refer to both freedom in general and national independence. Yet this term also expresses the Buddhist concept of spiritual deliverance, the end of the cycle of rebirths and the reaching of nirvana ... Thus, Buddhist notions of freedom or independence, unity, and mental culture (in the sense of meditation) formed the ideological thread of Aung San's conception of the nation.'[13]

Asked by Alan Clements what Buddhist meditation meant to *her*, Suu Kyi summed it up as 'a form of spiritual cultivation – a spiritual education and a purifying process'. 'Purity of mind' was what she had been striving – and was still striving – for, she said. That, and 'personal perfection'.[14]

The same question, put to her colleague U Tin Oo –
former Commander-in-Chief of the Armed Forces,
co-founder of the NLD and veteran political prisoner –
elicited a rather more visceral response.

Describing his first term in solitary confinement, the
decorated war hero recalled the sensation of being in a
pressure cooker on the cusp of explosion. Stricken with
severe dysentery, doubled over with pain and rage, 'I sat
down on the floor of my cell and felt like I was going to
weep.' He had with him a small primer on meditation by
the great *vipassanā* adept, the Mahasi Sayadaw. He
followed its instructions on the practice. 'If it's pain, be
aware of pain. If it's joy, well, just be aware of joy, and so
forth ... After the first ten minutes or so the anger and
pain increased. I said, "This is only creating more pain."
But I stayed with it and after an hour or so, it was like a
miracle ... the pain and anger simply disappeared ... I
now had a friend in prison, myself, my mindfulness.'[15]

Dr Ma Thida, another prominent dissident who also
'went to Moscow' (a euphemism for doing time in Insein
Prison), went on to write about her marathon *vipassanā*
sessions of twenty hours as a process of death and rebirth.
'Why not take advantage of being in prison to change my
life and get out of the cycle to find total liberation?' she
reasoned. 'Not physical freedom but total freedom.'[16]

Suu Kyi was quick to point out that house arrest in
one's family home was not quite the same as solitary

confinement in a nefarious prison like Insein. 'When people say: "How marvellous it is that you stuck out those six years of detention," my reaction is, "Well, what's so difficult about it? What's all the fuss about?" Anybody can stick out six years of house arrest. It's those people who have had to stick out years and years in prison, in terrible conditions, that make you wonder how they did it.'[17]

She seldom let on that her own episodes of house arrest were no picnic either. She rarely spoke of how at one point she stopped eating because she didn't want any handouts from her captors; how she was reduced to selling off some of her furniture in order to buy her own food; how she fell ill and grew terribly thin and began losing hair by the handful. She didn't like drama, was the way she put it. 'I suppose it would be a lot more dramatic if one were taken from one's home and put into a prison cell and the doors went clang,' she allowed. 'But it was not like that with me.'[18]

The doors had gone clang on a great many of her NLD supporters, among them leaders of the '88 Generation', student activists who had been at the forefront of the 1988 uprising. Those who escaped death in the ensuing military crackdown were either huddled in a makeshift jungle camp at the borderlands, doomed to malaria and failure, or behind bars in some unspeakable prison, doomed to torture and failure. Many would serve out sentences of fifteen years on average, some for such crimes as distributing pamphlets calling for the release of Aung San Suu Kyi.

She was now free; they weren't. What did freedom feel like, Clements wanted to know. As with all questions that touched on the inner life – where vulnerability, doubt and pain reside – her answer was unyielding. 'So many journalists have asked me, "How did you feel when you were released?" I have said, "I felt nothing at all." [Laughing] I had a vague idea that I should feel something, but ... the point was, well, what do I do now?'[19]

Yes, what exactly was Aung San Suu Kyi, celebrated prisoner of conscience, Nobel Prize laureate, crusader for democracy, going to do now that she was free? What manifesto might be forthcoming from the leader of the only credible opposition party, the NLD? What were her thoughts on foreign policy, on America's response to, or role in, Burma's struggle for democracy? These were the kinds of questions being put to her not only by Clements, but by other Western journalists and interlocutors. And these were the kinds of answers they were getting:

'As you know, I never discuss our future plans.'[20]

'I am not interested in trying to predict the future. What we are trying to do is shape the kind of future that we want for our country. And that comes about through endeavour.'

To a follow-up question about whether the NLD shouldn't be putting forward a viable plan for running the country in the event of regime change, her response was: 'We don't have a rigid view of what we want for Burma. We are a political party that represents the people of Burma. In fact, I can say that we are the only organisation in Burma that has received a mandate of the people. So there is a lot that we have to do.'[21]

Over the next few years, Suu Kyi did in fact manage to do a lot despite steady interference and harassment from the State Law & Order Restoration Council, the ruling junta, better known by its hapless acronym, SLORC. She toured the country, giving speeches and pep talks to adoring crowds. She preached democracy, self-reliance and non-violence, always in keeping with Buddhist ideals and beliefs, with the struggle for *loki nibbana*, or a utopian society in the mundane world, that would require a 'revolution of the spirit'. The overlap between spiritual and political aspirations was natural, she maintained, and would remain 'part of the design of our lives', for 'politics is about people, and you can't separate people from their spiritual values'.[22]

On weekends she would appear over the finials of her iron gate, flanked by her two senior party stalwarts, U Tin Oo and U Kyi Maung, to engage in impromptu conversations with regular crowds. The anthropologist Christina Fink, one of the few Western observers present at the 'People's Forums', as they came to be called, describes the kind of excitement they generated.

When the NLD leaders arrived at the gate, everyone would leap up, shouting and clapping ecstatically ... Once I made the mistake of sitting next to a wizened old man, long past seventy and missing most of his teeth. When Daw Aung San Suu Kyi appeared, he was so eager to signal his approval that he jumped to his feet and proceeded to twirl his umbrella over his head faster and faster, endangering the lives of all sitting around him. He had to be gently restrained ...[23]

The three personages took turns speaking – about democracy and human rights and freedom. But it was for Aung San Suu Kyi that the crowds had come: to hang on her every word, to laugh and cheer with abandon, to applaud her aphorisms – empowering adages like 'All things change eventually, even the government of Burma'; and 'Your heads are not only for nodding "yes"'; and, of course, 'Fear is a habit.'

On 30 May 2003, while on tour of the Depayin district north of Mandalay, Suu Kyi and her entourage were set upon by paramilitary thugs in an attack that left scores of NLD supporters dead and hundreds arrested. Suu Kyi was taken into 'protective custody' and escorted back to Rangoon, to be placed once more under house arrest. There she remained until November 2010.

4.

In 1990, Myanmar was visited by a marvellous phenomenon. Buddha statues across the country began developing a swelling on their left breasts.[24] Unlike the Ganesha miracle that would take India by storm a few years later – when statues of elephant-headed deities in Hindu temples began sipping milk by the spoonful from pilgrims – the Buddha-breast miracle in Myanmar was indicative of milk-giving – not milk-taking – in the foundational Buddhist sense. According to one early legend of the Buddha's life:

The Buddha has arrived in heaven and is seated under a tree surrounded by a vast assembly of disciples. In a lengthy discourse, he relates stories of his birth and expresses the wish to see again the sublime face of his mother. A messenger swiftly relays this message to Maya [his birth mother] some distance away. Upon hearing her son's words, milk streams from her breasts. Overwhelmed with emotion, she responds that if he is indeed her son, her milk will reach his mouth directly. And so, miraculously, her milk enters his mouth from afar.[25]

Be that as it may, the phenomenon of the Buddha's breast swelling in 1990 was seen as an omen favourable to Aung San Suu Kyi's political ascendancy, coinciding as it did with her party's astounding landslide victory in the elections that year, the first to be held in two decades of military rule. As the entrenched junta proceeded to annul the results while continuing to imprison the party's leader, Suu Kyi and her non-violent struggle against military oppression were soon elevated to the realm of mystery and prodigy, where signs and omens flourished. People began seeing her as 'a heroine like the mythical mother goddess of the earth who can free them from the enslavement of the evil military captors'.[26] She was an angel; she was a saint; she was a female Bodhisattva.

Suu Kyi was usually the first to brush aside any attributions of divinity: 'Oh, for goodness' sake, I'm nowhere near such a state.'[27] She was no saint, no magician, she insisted. She was just an ordinary person going about her business, seeking personal perfection while trying to lead her people on the path to salvation through a revolution of the spirit. What was all the fuss and drama about? She didn't like drama, she kept saying.

Still, it was one particular drama, the stuff of archetype and myth, that qualified her for the ultimate sanctification as Mother Suu, Matriarch of Myanmar.

Early on during her long stint under house arrest, it became clear to Suu Kyi that she would have to choose between country and family. For a while it seemed possible for her sons Alexander and Kim, and her husband Michael, to at least travel from England to visit her from time to time. But ultimately they were at the mercy of military officialdom, which was not in the habit of granting mercy visas, even to the families of high-profile political prisoners. The authorities let it be known that Suu Kyi herself was free to leave the country anytime she wanted, but with no guarantee that she would be allowed back in.

'My main reaction was surprise that they ever thought that I would take up such an offer,' was her response. 'It indicated that they did not know me at all.'[28] After her release in 2010, she told the BBC: 'There never was a point when I thought of going. I knew that I wouldn't go. And he [Michael] knew too.'[29]

Michael had been put on notice from the early days of their courtship. In her by now famous response to his marriage proposal in 1972, she wrote: 'I only ask one thing, that should my people need me, you would help me to do my duty by them. Would you mind very much

41

should such a situation arise? How probable it is I do not know, but the possibility is there.'[30]

In the spring of 1991 I met Michael Aris for lunch at Harvard, where he was Visiting Professor of Tibetology. I had never met Aung San Suu Kyi, so when the inevitable subject of this letter came up I asked if it had surprised him at the time. I was referring to what seemed to me an oddly decorous tone for a love letter ('should my people need me ... Would you mind very much ...'). But Michael, misunderstanding my question, said he wasn't at all surprised: he had always known how much Suu's country meant to her. It was a moment, I realised, when he was lobbying internationally for her recognition as a political prisoner who was not just duty-bound but *destined* to lead. A few weeks later he rang me to say that she'd won the Nobel Peace Prize.

In 1997 Michael was diagnosed with prostate cancer. The question then was whether his wife would be allowed to see him. As Michael's illness worsened, appeals to the military regime to grant him a visa were made by heads of state and world leaders like Pope John Paul II and UN Secretary-General Kofi Annan – all to no avail. Suu Kyi remained intransigent throughout, curtly turning down offers by the authorities to facilitate a visit for her to Britain.

Michael died in 1999, leaving Alexander and Kim bereft of both parents. But still their mother refused to leave Burma and risk being shut out of the country. By then, the boys were no strangers to their mother's formidable strength of purpose. They had been with her in Rangoon during her first house arrest, when she went on a hunger strike. In his biography of Aung San Suu Kyi, veteran journalist Bertil Lintner makes the point that hunger strikes, when intended as political acts, do require management. Suu Kyi's was 'perhaps inspired by Gandhi, but he went on hunger strikes in the full view of the masses of people around him for maximum impact on the public at large and the international community. Many would argue that going on a hunger strike while under detention has little propaganda value and only inflicts suffering on the person refusing to eat.'[31]

Presumably also on the children of the person refusing to eat? 'We don't go in for melodrama in our family,' said Suu Kyi. 'We just think of the practical aspect of it. I do not encourage melodrama. I don't like it ... I just think melodrama is very silly. One has to live life on an even keel.'[32]

'But what about the simplicity of pure emotions without melodrama?' her interviewer persisted. 'Well, there is nothing to get emotional about,' she pointed out. 'And how is getting emotional going to help? It just uses up more energy.'[33] Of course she missed her sons. 'One wants to be together with one's family. That's what fami-lies are about. There are things that you do together that you don't do with other people. It's very special.'[34] And of course she had regrets. *Personal* regrets, even. But then, Aung San Suu Kyi has never been one to publicly express any doubts about the choices she's made.

That she stuck to her guns even as her husband was dying went on to become the subject of much discussion and interpretation, striking many outside Myanmar as almost impossible to credit. 'This woman has no human-ity,' one reader of the *New York Times* commented. To which a Burmese person responded, 'She chose her sick country over her sick husband. It's called sacrifice. You see it as lacking humanity, but I see it as full of human-ity.'[35] Even more humane and altruistic in the eyes of her compatriots was a mother's readiness to renounce her sons for the greater good of her nation. Could any sacri-fice be more selfless? After all, while 'the idea of amassing surplus wealth, or hoarding, was repugnant to the Burmese Buddhist mind ... it delighted in giving and surrendering, in emulation of the Buddha-to-be, Wethandaya [Vessantara in Pali], who gave up not only his throne but his children as well to a mendicant.'[36]

To Aung San Suu Kyi, self-sacrifice of that order was but an expression of the love called for both in the Bible ('perfect love casts out fear') and in the *metta sutta*, the Buddhist discourses of loving-kindness, where 'we have the phrase, "like a mother caring for her only child". That's true *metta*. A mother's courage to sacrifice herself comes out of her love for her child. And I think we need a lot more of this kind of love around the place.'[37]

In her examination of what she calls 'the mothering path', the Buddhist scholar Pascale Engelmajer points out that 'mothering work, in its different iterations, is an intentional activity, repeated day after day for the sake of many. The motivations that it is based on, compassion and loving-kindness, *are* the foundation of the Buddhist path ... mothering activities serve not only as metaphors for the Buddha and his teachings, but as models for action and for the development of these virtues.'[38]

In recent years, innumerable odes to Mother Suu have been declaimed in public and posted on social media in Myanmar, in language embracing the sentimental and the nonsensical, often at the same time.

The dark nights of an evil past
lasted far too long, mother.

When you hear dogs baying in the dark
Night don't get up, mother,
it could rob you of your sleep, I fear ...

Thanks to a mother's love
can entire Myanmar
let flowers bloom instead of bullets.[39]

I do not talk of romantic love. The love I speak of is
very maternal, pure and clean, peaceful. We are not
reciting a poem but celebrating a convocation. A
degree is given to scholars who have learnt the
subject. Now a convocation for the doctorate degree
of a mother's love for the nation![40]

On Facebook, posts and pages removed since the 2021
coup spoke of Aung San Suu Kyi 'teaching her beloved
countrymen in a very short period what the essence of
democracy really is' and lamented her sons' deprivation
of 'the warmth of her bosom'.

For all her eloquence on the loving-kindness of *metta*,
and the perfect love that casts out fear and conquers all,
Aung San Suu Kyi remained stoic and long-suffering
about one of the great loves of her life: the army. It was
her father, after all, the other great love of her life, who
founded the Burmese army – the Tatmadaw, (Royal
Army), as it now calls itself. From her very first tussles
with the military leaders, and all through her serial
detentions and reprieves, Suu Kyi never missed an
opportunity to declare her devotion to the very institu-
tion that proclaimed her an enemy of the state.

'I have a rapport with the army,' she said. 'As a child I was cared for by [my father's] soldiers. I was brought up to regard them as friends.'[41] As a child, she even wanted to dress like a general. After all, her earliest memories of her father were of him in uniform.[42] And when she had children of her own, her enduring romance with the military would find expression in little family rituals, like baking a birthday cake for her son in the shape of a tank.[43]

'I have always been very fond of the military,' she repeated in more than one interview. Coming on the heels of a long stint under house arrest, such statements were met with understandable scepticism. What was behind them? Stockholm syndrome? Sweet talk to disarm the enemy and dispel any intentions of retribution?

No, it was love pure and simple, she insisted. Love unconditional. For even if, as an advocate of non-violence, she believed that those who resorted to violence were 'undermining the very foundations of human rights ... if you love someone, you love them in spite of themselves and you hope they'll redeem themselves'.[44] She didn't believe in 'taking the kind of action that will destroy people for what they have done in the past. I believe in people's right to redeem themselves.'[45]

* * *

Suu Kyi's devotion to the military makes for a rousing love story, but one bound to end in tears, seeing that the love has gone unrequited. Earlier I mentioned Homer's Helen of Troy, whose beauty makes old men rise to their feet. Those same old men, Trojan elders who greet Helen at the Scaean Gate, can't wait to see the back of her.

> Just like a goddess,
> immortal, awe-inspiring. She's beautiful.
> But nonetheless let her go back with the ships.
> Let her not stay here, a blight on us, our children.

The Tatmadaw elders back in 1996 were similarly sick and fed up with their beautiful, awe-inspiring nemesis, and they put it to her in the prosody of a *New Light of Myanmar* column. 'You had better leave this nation. As citizens, we are demanding deportation of Mrs Aris. The only word we have to say to you is "Get out."[46]

Another epithet for Mrs Aris was *Anauk Medawgyi*, the name of a particular *nat* (ghost persona) in the pantheon of Burmese folk spirits. *Anauk Medawgyi* means 'Great Mother of the West' – another oblique reference to Suu Kyi's foreign leanings.

This was not exactly the same mother figure venerated by the masses as Amay Suu, Mother of all Myanmar. And here was the problem. Because, as the old military slogan made clear, when it came to the nation's parentage,

Only the army is mother
Only the army is father

Not so for the nation's children. For the people of
Myanmar, only Amay Suu was mother, and only she
could save them from an abusive fake father, the
Tatmadaw. Amay Suu had all the virtues so woefully lacking in the generals claiming paternity: beauty, pedigree,
courage, intelligence, grace, refinement. Amay Suu
brimmed with *awza*, that inborn moral authority of the
great; the Tatmadaw knew only *ana*, the authority of
brute power and merciless might. Amay Suu fostered the
loving kindness of *metta*; the Tatmadaw had only ever
brought *dukkha* to the people.

The word *dukkha* – commonly translated as 'suffering'
or 'pain' – seems especially apt in this context. The Pali
word derives from the Sanskrit, a language brought to
India by the ancient Aryans, a nomadic people who trav-
elled in horse- or ox-drawn vehicles. Joseph Goldstein,
the American *vipassanā* scholar, explains the etymology
nicely: '*Dukkha* is made up of the prefix *du* and the root
kha. Du means "bad" or "difficult". *Kha* means "empty"
... One of the specific meanings [of 'empty'] refers to the
empty axle hole of a wheel. If the axle fits badly into the
center hole, we get a very bumpy ride. This is a good
analogy for our ride through the cycle of rebirth, the
saṃsāra.[47]

A good analogy too for the Tatmadaw: those insuffera-
ble axle holes.

The long contest for parental supremacy between Aung
San Suu Kyi and the military junta took a radical turn in
2012. After a good seven decades of military dictatorship,
'Dad's Army' was ready to make concessions. After a
good third of her life in detention, Mother Suu was at last
set free. The parties entered into an agreement of shared
custody. The probationary plan was called the 7-Step
Roadmap to Discipline-Flourishing Democracy. Together
they would set out their vision for the future of their
child, the Burmese nation.

Mother Suu was back in the game, although, as everyone
knew, the cards were firmly stacked in favour of the
ruling junta. Under their constitution, specifically rewrit-
ten in 2008 to bar her from the presidency, the military
still controlled a quarter of all parliamentary seats, and
any changes to the constitution required the votes of
three-quarters of the legislators plus one.

Nevertheless, democracy, that long-cherished pipe
dream of the populace, was now the politically sanctioned catchword of the new government. Aung San Suu
Kyi became a member of parliament. Reforms and
amnesties followed, palpable and dramatic. Hundreds of
political prisoners were released. Labour laws were

amended to allow unions and strikes. Press censorship was lifted and freedom of speech rules were relaxed. Revised currency and banking regulations made for overnight economic liberalisation.

The world could be forgiven for thinking that Myanmar might, just might, be on its way to achieving a form of democracy – even if Suu Kyi warned repeatedly that the country had a long way to go before the real thing came to pass.

Meanwhile, military parliamentarians had their own concerns about the perversions taking place in the name of democracy. When in 2016 the NLD managed to pass legislation creating a new post for Aung San Suu Kyi as State Counsellor of Myanmar, making her the de facto head of government, one of the generals with a seat in parliament accused the NLD of 'democratic bullying'.[48] But as Amay Suu came to be seen as the face of civilian government, her governing style would be called 'democratic dictatorship' – and not only by critics within the military. Increasingly, words like 'imperious', 'aloof', 'cold' and 'out of touch' were churned out by the rumour mills.[49]

Other dictatorial traits were more worrying: 'Legislators complain that Suu Kyi personally makes all important decisions; their own roles seem trivial by comparison, and the idea of voting against the government is unheard of. Even high-ranking officials wait for her to weigh in on issues well within their areas of responsibility. The results are bottlenecks and even virtual paralysis despite an urgent need to make decisions. Suu Kyi's domination of the NLD has another troubling side effect. She is seventy-two years old, but has made no known arrangements for a successor or a generational changing of the guard.'[50]

But these were the mutterings of professional malcontents, and almost all of them were foreigners. For the Bamar people, who form the ethnic majority population, Aung San Suu Kyi was their one and only Mother Suu. Among the ethnic minority population, on the other hand, Amay Suu did not command quite the same allegiance. Wars between the EAO's (Ethnic Armed Organisations) and the central government had persisted since independence, and while the so-called transition to democracy and the promises of the NLD government had raised high hopes for a genuine multi-ethnic Union of Myanmar, such hopes were fading fast – as was the mystique of Mother Suu – in the ethnic-minority provinces.

As far as her Bamar children were concerned, however, Aung San Suu Kyi and the NLD were the only pathfinders worth following on the road to democracy. Who cared if more than two-thirds of the population still lived without electricity, and even the privileged remaining third had to put up with routine power outages? Who cared if the nation's roads and trains were still a disgrace, and public transport ever a mess? Who cared if the ethnic minorities, accounting for more than a third of Myanmar's population, were still forced to live in perennial war zones, in what was widely known as 'the longest-lasting civil war of our times'? Amay Suu was doing her best to restore peace and harmony through such tireless initiatives as 'national reconciliation', 'union spirit' and 'Nationwide Ceasefire Agreements'. She had given the people her word that she would go on working for democracy 'for as long as I'm alive or until we get it'.[51]

Aung San Suu Kyi and the NLD would go on to win two successive national elections, in 2015 and 2020 – both by landslides. But to the world at large, neither vote was as startling as the show of support for Myanmar's Mother Suu in her decision in December 2019 to appear in person at the International Court of Justice at The Hague.

Suu Kyi was taking it upon herself, as State Counsellor and Foreign Minister of Myanmar, to defend her country from charges of genocide committed against the Rohingya, the predominantly Muslim ethnic minority in the western state of Rakhine. Filed by the Gambia on behalf of the Organisation of Islamic Cooperation, the landmark lawsuit accused Myanmar of 'genocidal acts' and other atrocities that had driven three-quarters of a million Rohingya from their homes in Rakhine into neighbouring Bangladesh, where they remained trapped in dire refugee settlements.

Suu Kyi's willingness to take the stand at the ICJ hearings, when she could have let the generals themselves take the heat – after all, it was their military operations that carried out the 'textbook case of ethnic cleansing', as the UN called it – marked the final collapse of her international reputation. Over the previous several years, her refusal to criticise the generals on matters of human rights violations and to speak out in defence of the Rohingya, a blatantly persecuted and disenfranchised people, had earned her the opprobrium of the international community. One by one, the honours and awards once showered upon the celebrated beacon of democracy and defender of human rights were stripped away and taken back. There were calls for her Nobel Peace Prize to be rescinded.

Addressing his fellow Peace Prize laureate as 'dear sister', Desmond Tutu, the South African anti-apartheid activist, appealed to Suu Kyi to put principle above political expediency. 'If the political price of your ascension to the highest office in Myanmar is your silence, the price is surely too steep', he remonstrated in an open letter, urging her to intervene in the 'ethnic cleansing' and 'slow genocide'.

It wasn't of course within Suu Kyi's power to intervene in military operations, so she couldn't be held responsible for the excesses of an army on the march, even one she was brought up to think of as family. Nonetheless, some public expression of sympathy for the victims of such egregious human rights abuses seemed called for. But no such sentiment was forthcoming.

Instead, when asked by an American student who the Rohingya were and why they were being persecuted in Myanmar, Suu Kyi's reply was, 'You should not use emotive words like persecution. What had happened was that there was communal violence. There were crimes committed by both communities.'[52] On another occasion, during a panel at the London School of Economics, a similar question – why Aung San Suu Kyi hadn't condemned the recent Burmese military offensive in Kachin State that had displaced 80,000 people – elicited similar evasion: 'Resolving conflict is not about condemnation, it is about finding out the root, the cause of the conflict.'[53]

Under the circumstances, Aung San Suu Kyi's appearance at the ICJ was seen by a great many in Myanmar as a patriot's mission to defend her nation's honour – to make genocide look respectable, as George Orwell might have put it.

In the days preceding the hearings in The Hague, Mother Suu mania took the form of widespread campaign fever. All across Myanmar, and among Burmese communities overseas, rallies gathered steam. A Facebook event dubbed 'We Stand with Aung San Suu Kyi' invited social media participation. Travel agencies announced special 'Law and Leisure' packages to The Hague, where one could sit in on the ICJ court sessions when not touring local 'tourist hotspots'. Shared buses and accommodation in The Hague were arranged for the exiled communities in London and Paris.

On 10 December, when the hearings began, thousands of citizens thronged the city hall square in Yangon and thousands more flocked to other hubs across the country, all brandishing flags, banners and placards with Aung San Suu Kyi's image and 'We Stand with Aung San Suu Kyi' legends.

Inside the courtroom at The Hague, according to *The Guardian*, 'Aung San Suu Kyi sat in the front row, her hands resting on a table. As a list of atrocities was read out she stared ahead at the raised bank of judges in front of her, her face expressionless. With accusations accumulating, her body appeared to tense and her rapidly blinking eyes glanced occasionally up towards the courtroom's stained-glass windows and chandeliers.'[54]

In line with the charge of 'genocidal intent', the prosecutors described how Tatmadaw soldiers set houses on fire, including those with people in them; how other victims were forced inside houses that were then set alight; how babies were wrenched from their mothers and flung to the ground, or into the river, or onto open fires and burned alive; how mass gang rapes were carried out in military and police compounds, and in open public spaces while family and neighbours were forced to watch, how women who had been raped, pregnant women among them, suffered further mutilation to their breasts and genitals.[55]

Myanmar's labyrinthine citizenship laws preclude full citizenship rights for the Rohingya, an ethnic minority not listed among the 135 official indigenous groups recognised by the government. Suu Kyi herself refused to acknowledge the Rohingya by name. Doing so would have meant acknowledging their legitimacy in her national family, thereby infuriating her 'legitimate' family of Buddhist nationalists, whose kindest name for the Rohingya was 'Bengali'. That the Rohingya insisted on calling themselves Rohingya was taken by their militant Bamar brethren as further evidence of illegitimacy – although, as the anthropologist Jane Ferguson points out, 'The volatility and hotly contested nature of the "Rohingya" issue ... raises questions as to whether it would even be within the bounds of strategic essentialism to call oneself Rohingya in such a politically charged climate.'[56]

In her closing speech, Suu Kyi allowed that 'It cannot be ruled out that disproportionate force was used in some cases by defence forces', but argued that 'genocidal intent cannot be the only hypothesis'.[57] What other hypotheses might be construed was difficult to imagine, given the wording of the UN report: 'The actions of those who orchestrated the attacks on the Rohingya read as a veritable check-list' of what a state would have done had it 'wished to destroy the target group in whole or in part'.[58]

'If war crimes have been committed,' was all Suu Kyi would concede, 'they will be prosecuted within our military justice system.'[59]

In raising the question of her complicity in the crimes enumerated, the lead lawyer for Gambia's prosecution team held up a picture of large billboards that had appeared in Myanmar in recent days, showing Aung San Suu Kyi superimposed in front of three smiling generals with the caption: 'We Stand With You'.

On 14 December, when she returned to Naypyidaw, the crowds lining the road from the airport welcomed her home with flags, banners and posters, many of which read 'We Stand With Amay Suu' – but minus the generals.

A year later, in November 2020, Aung San Suu Kyi and the NLD won the national elections by a landslide. A few months after the election, the day the new government was scheduled to assume office on 1 February 2021, General Min Aung Hlaing declared his takeover of power in a coup d'état.

Aung San Suu Kyi was back in prison – this time on charges that could warrant a 125-year prison sentence.

Within days of the coup, carnival had come to Yangon. The crowds, overwhelmingly young and defiant, were out in force to protest the military takeover, brandishing slogans and demands with one hand, raising three-finger salutes[60] with the other. They sang, they chanted, they declaimed and versified, turning the city into one big jamboree.

Strutting their stuff in fanciful processions were transgender warriors from the demi-monde of spirit worship; bare-chested musclemen and bodybuilders; women flaunting, in defiance of gender taboos, barricades made from sarongs, and bloodied menstrual pads stuck onto images of General Min Aung Hlaing; lawyers with emoji mask disguises; women in white doctor's coats or bridal gowns; a parade of uncanny Aung San Suu Kyi lookalikes ...

Protest as street theatre was only the prelude to what came to be known as the Spring Revolution, an entertaining and peaceful – that is to say, unarmed – Mardi Gras. As demonstrations and rallies spread from cities to towns to villages across the country, with millions eventually taking to the street; as tens of thousands of state employees, healthcare workers, shopkeepers and other civilians staged CDM (Civil Disobedience Movement) boycotts and strikes, the revolution evolved in unexpected ways.

On placards and street signs, on social media posts and feeds, came the mea culpa of Bamar people expressing shame for the decades of discrimination they inflicted on their ethnic minority brethren. They apologised especially to the Rohingya for ignoring, denying or condoning their suffering at the hands of the Bamar military. In return, from refugee camps in Bangladesh, and from within Myanmar where some still remained, Rohingya sympathisers expressed solidarity through three-finger salutes and their own watchwords of wisdom: 'Dark skin, OK. Dark history, not OK.'

It was a moment of truth and reconciliation at a pop-up peace congress, stoking catchwords like *federalism*, new calls for *accountability* and *power-sharing*, a renewed common purpose: *Down with the Military!*

The inevitable crackdown by security forces began less than a week later, with tear gas and water cannons leading to the shooting and killing of unarmed civilians; to midnight raids and manhunts; to the burning of houses and clinics and entire neighbourhoods; to arrests and disappearances ending in trials by torture and summary beheadings. Throughout it all, a popular slogan kept making the rounds on social media. Attributed to Pablo Neruda, the quote had done service in Cairo, during another, earlier, Spring Revolution: *You can cut all the flowers, but you cannot stop the spring.*

The hashtag #WhatsHappeningInMyanmar serves as an index finger on the pulse of developments since the coup. 'Hope is rare now in Myanmar' said a statement in March 2023 from the UN High Commissioner for Human Rights.[61] 'By nearly every feasible measurement, and in every area of human rights – economic, social and cultural, as much as civil and political – Myanmar has profoundly regressed.'[62] Other international rights groups and news sources provide detailed estimated break-downs of the coup and its wreckage: more than 3,000 people killed by regime forces. Nearly 17,000 still under detention. At least 55,000 civilian structures burned to the ground. 1.2 million people internally displaced. 17.6 million in need of humanitarian aid. Close to 50 per cent of the population living below the poverty line. According to the World Food Programme (WFP), '13.2 million do not know where their next meal will come from and the food that they do get is insufficient in meeting their nutritional needs'.[63]

In December 2022, an eighteen-month succession of closed trials in Naypyidaw was finally brought to an end. Charged with a barrage of crimes, from the felony of having unregistered walkie-talkies, to corruption (accepting bribes), to violating the Covid-19 restrictions, to approving the illegal purchase and lease of a helicopter,

Aung San Suu Kyi was sentenced to thirty-three years in prison. Unlike her previous incarcerations, however, prison this time bespeaks solitary confinement on a military base, with none of the amenities of house arrest or even of Yangon's notorious Insein Jail.[64]

So far, as of March 2023, there is no indication that Myanmar's pre-eminent political prisoner will ever be set free in this lifetime. She turns seventy-seven in June 2023.

A martyr's life is cut short in glorious sacrifice. General Aung San, martyred not as a soldier but as a statesman with a vision for a free, democratic Burma, passed on the torch to his daughter, who through her loving kindness and sacrifice – not for the sole benefit of her immediate family, but for that of her nation and everybody who is seen to belong to it – took on the task of mothering Myanmar. That, in short, is the way Aung San Suu Kyi is perceived by the majority of her Buddhist compatriots.

According to the Theravada Buddhist world view, the child is forever indebted to the mother for her sacrifice of giving life, nourishment and care in the womb and thereafter. Boys become monks for that fundamental reason: to repay their mother's *metta*, her loving kindness. They make merit on their mother's behalf to ensure a higher rebirth for her.

Without sharing the same meritorious intention toward Amay Suu, the military regime has ensured for Aung San Suu Kyi a higher earthly stature, if not a higher rebirth, by elevating her to martyrdom. This will confer even greater *awza* for *Kaungkin Maymay* (Heavenly Mama), as some of her devotees call her – as she presides over a new generation of sacrificial sons and daughters and assumes the national mantle of *Martyr Familias*.

Special thanks to
Jane Ferguson and Bertil Lintner

Notes

1. 'Amnesty's Rights Generation', www.youtube.com/watch?v=CbD6_YMGk4E
2. https://www.amnesty.org/en/latest/news/2018/11/amnesty-withdraws-award-from-aung-san-suu-kyi/
3. *Time*, 12 July 2013 https://world.time.com/2013/07/12/aung-san-suu-kyi-produces-her-fathers-biopic-but-dont-expect-miracles/
4. Aung San Suu Kyi, *Freedom from Fear: And Other Writings* (London: Penguin Books, 1995), xviii
5. Ba Maw, *Breakthrough in Burma: Memoirs of a Revolution, 1939–1946* (New Haven: Yale University Press, 1968), 65
6. UK Parliament, House of Commons Debate, 5 November 1947
7. Pe Maung Tin, *The Path of Purity: Buddhaghosa's Visuddhimagga* (London: Oxford University Press, 1931), Part II, 113

8. Alan Clements, *The Voice of Hope* (New York: Seven Stories Press, 1997), 230

9. Aung San Suu Kyi, 193

10. Clements, 209

11. Aung San Suu Kyi Commencement Address, American University, Winter 1997 (delivered in absentia): https://dra.american.edu/islandora/object/auislandora:65188

12. David Marr, *Vietnamese Tradition on Trial, 1920–1945* (Berkeley and Los Angeles: University of California Press, 1981), 308

13. Gustaaf Houtman, 'Mental Culture in Burmese Crisis Politics: Aung San Suu Kyi and the National League for Democracy' (*Institute for the Study of Languages and Cultures of Asia and Africa, Tokyo University of Foreign Studies, Monograph series 33*), 34

14. Clements, 49, 76, 77, 92

15. Clements, 290

16. *The Bangkok Post*, 17 September 2016

17. Clements, 67

18. Clements, 211

19. Clements, 114

20. Clements, 102

21. Ron Gluckman, 'The Lady and the Tramps': https://www.gluckman.com/AungSanSuuKyi.html

22. Clements, 39

23. Christina Fink, *Living Silence: Burma Under Military Rule* (New York: Zed Books, 2001), 88

24. Mya Maung, *Totalitarianism in Burma: Prospects for Economic Development* (New York: Paragon House, 1992), 184

25. Wendy Garling, 'Three Forgotten Stories About the Buddha's Mother', *Tricycle*, 12 MAY 2017 https://tricycle.org/trikedaily/three-forgotten-stories-buddhas-mother/

26. Mya Maung, 163

27. Clements, 28

28. Clements, 136, 143

29. BBC News, 23 September 2012: https://www.bbc.com/news/magazine-19667956

30. Aung San Suu Kyi, xix

31. Bertil Lintner, *Aung San Suu Kyi and Burma's Struggle for Democracy* (Chiangmai: Silkworm Books, 2011), 77, 78

32. Clements, 131

33. Clements, 132

34. BBC News, https://www.bbc.com/news/magazine-19667956

35. *The New York Times*, 2 February 2021

36. E.M. Law-Yone, *The Monarchies of Burma* (unpublished manuscript)

37. Clements, 38

38. Pascale Engelmajer, 'Like a Mother Her Only Child:

Mothering in the Pāli Canon', *Open Theology 2020*; 6), 102

39. Hans-Bernd Zöllner and Rodion Ebbighausen, *The Daughter: A Political Biography of Aung San Suu Kyi* (Chiangmai: Silkworm Books, 2018), 217, 218

40. Maung Than Yu, https://www.poetryfoundation.org/harriet-books/2014/05/a-ministry-of-defense-but-no-ministry-of-peace-a-celebration-of-myanmar-poetry-at-the-irrawaddy-literary-festival

41. *The New York Times*, 11 January 1989

42. Clements, 55, 56

43. *Desert Island Discs*, BBC Radio 4, 27 January 2013

44. Amnesty's Rights Generation", www.youtube.com/watch?v=CbD6_YMGk4E

45. World Economic Forum, 'Myanmar: What Future?', 11 June 2013: https://www.youtube.com/watch?v=ADQSqUBZjvE

46. Monique Skidmore, ed. *Burma at the Turn of the Twenty-first Century*, (Honolulu:University of Hawai'i Press, 2005), 142

47. Joseph Goldstein, *Mindfulness: A Practical Guide to Awakening* Boulder CO: (Sounds True, 2013), 376

48. Zoltan Barany, 'Burma: Suu Kyi's Missteps', *Journal of Democracy*, vol. 29, no. 1, Jan. 2018, 16

49. These and similar opinions were expressed to me privately by journalists, politicians, political prisoners and activists who had either known Aung

San Suu Kyi personally or known close relatives or associates of hers. These sources must remain anonymous, especially since the 2021 coup

50. Barany, 8

51. Clements, 61

52. 'Amnesty's Rights Generation', www.youtube.com/watch?v=CbD6_YMGk4E

53. *Kachinland News*, 25 June 2012, https://www.kachinlandnews.com/?p=21965

54. *The Guardian*, 10 December 2019

55. UN Human Rights Council, Report of the detailed findings of the Independent International Fact-Finding Mission on Myanmar, UN Doc. A/HRC/39/CRP.2 (17 Sept. 2018)

56. Jane M.Ferguson, 2015. 'Who's Counting? Ethnicity, Belonging, and the National Census in Burma/Myanmar.' *Bijdragen tot de Taal-, Land- en Volkenkunde*. (171): 1–28

57. ICJ Verbatim Record, https://www.icj-cij.org/public/files/case-related/178/178-20191211-ORA-01-00-BI.pdf

58. ICJ Verbatim Record, https://www.icj-cij.org/public/files/case-related/178/178-20191210-ORA-01-00-BI.pdf

59. ICJ Verbatim Record, https://www.icj-cij.org/public/files/case-related/178/178-20191210-ORA-01-00-BI.pdf, 18

60. Borrowed from the dystopian sci-fi movie *The Hunger Games*, the three-finger salute has been adopted by youthful anti-authoritarian movements in Thailand, Hong Kong, Taiwan and Myanmar

61. https://news.un.org/en/story/2023/03/1134247

62. https://www.ohchr.org/en/press-releases/2023/01/two-years-after-coup-myanmar-faces-unimaginable-regression-says-un-human

63. https://www.wfp.org/emergencies/myanmar-emergency

64. My source for this and other privileged information on Aung San Suu Kyi's whereabouts is Australian economist Sean Turnell, her close advisor until his own arrest and imprisonment by the military government. Also prosecuted under the Official Secrets Act, Turnell was sentenced to three years but released after twenty-two months. During their joint pre-trial court proceedings in Naypyidaw, he was able to see and speak to Suu Kyi – probably the last foreigner to do so since her most recent trials

Also from TLS Books

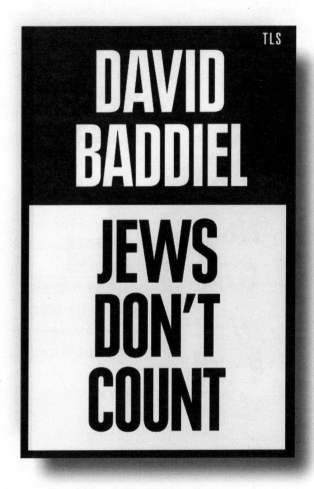

How identity politics failed one particular identity.

'The whole book is just brilliant –
and very much needed'
Simon Schama

Also from TLS Books

Lisa Hilton

Sex and the City of Ladies

*Rewriting history with Cleopatra,
Lucrezia Borgia and Catherine the Great*

Lisa Hilton picks up the mythical 'City of Ladies'
where the medieval writer Christine de Pisan
left off, continuing a conversation about gender
and greatness that began more than six hundred
years ago.